YOU CAN BEGIN AGAIN

REGAINING YOUR LIFE AFTER TRIALS AND DETOURS

BY

PRINCESS. N. SIZIBA

ISBN 978-1-77925-466-5

This book is a Publication of WING UP PUBLISHING

www.winguppublishing.com

info@winguppublishing.com

Cover design by: Run Ads

WING UP

PUBLISHING

Table of Contents

DEDICATION

To my dearest friend Jo Wynn. You were the voice that carried me through in my most challenging season and you showed me possibility where I saw a desert. Thank you for holding my hand and believing in me.

To every person who needs assurance that a new beginning is possible, this is for you. May you find the courage to begin again.

INTRODUCTION

On the 2nd of October 2019, I landed at OR Tambo airport with a pink suitcase full of broken dreams and dashed hopes. I had just flown half way across the world from a place considered to be the greatest land in the world, and was headed back to one of abject poverty and an atmosphere so rich in strife and futility. At thirty-three years old, unemployed and with a net worth that could fit in a suitcase, here 1 was heading back to my mother's house broken and distraught. A failure? Check! An embarrassment? Check! A nobody? Check! An underachiever? Check! An utter let down? Check! At this point I seemed to hold all the accolades of a write-off.

I also knew what I was coming back to, and I acknowledged the extraordinary strength I would have to amass, as well as the faith and mental fortitude I had to stir up to rebuild my life. I had done everything humanly possible to make my parents proud, and had also tried so hard to secure a better future for my daughter; but nothing I strove for worked. I was devastated...

My new name soon became misty eyes as 1 could barely see through the tears that washed my face every day. Without a choice, 1 found myself having to gather what was left of my pieces and build a meaningful life out of broken dreams. I had to begin again.

When I had finally reached a place of reasonable calm in my mind and emotions, the first thing I asked myself was; "what do 1 do with my broken dreams?" Out of that self-brooding came the consciousness that I could create new dreams out of those broken ones, I could begin again. I call it the moment of *coming to myself.* And so began the process of picking myself up from the gutter. It seemingly grew harder to get up each day, because each new day required new strength.

You see, when we pursue life or attempt something new, we are expectant of triumph and good success. We have expectations that the effort we exert in changing our lives should yield something. So when our dreams come crashing down, we never really know what to do with them. What do we do with our broken dreams and shattered pieces? It's factual that at times life will throw curveballs at us and we have no choice but to confront them, even with fear creeping up behind us like our own shadows.

Maybe you are thinking to yourself; "but how do 1 begin again?" You somehow feel closed in and are wondering how to start over and move forward. The divorce is final, the house has officially been repossessed. It has been confirmed that you are set out to be a single parent. You lost the job. The business did not take off. The one you called love is gone. You've survived the tragedy; so, what's next?

The reality is, in some moments we may not be able to immediately change our now, but we can alter our perspective on it in order to rise from it. So, we begin by shifting our viewpoint on life to focus on the positive that could possibly emerge out of our experiences. The reason why I say a shift in perception is needed is because, if you choose to look at something differently, it's as if you'll be seeing it for the very first time. Perspective matters.

This book is penned at a time when the world is dealing with a pandemic that no one saw coming. In a huff it just said; "1 am here!" For once we were all dealing with a common enemy. Dreams were interrupted, weddings were held off, home purchases tumbled, new business ventures were shelved, the global market weakened, hopes and dreams were deferred, and we all found ourselves having to become the people that the storm required to survive it. We had to be brave. I am not sure if there is anyone who can truthfully uphold that they have not been affected by this. Whether financially, emotionally or spiritually we have all had to make certain changes, the greatest of all being; "we had to begin again."

Even in all the chaos, broken dreams should not be the end, every new day is a chance to begin again. You can come out with purpose, a new heart, new strengths, molding experiences and abilities out of life's unexpected trials. You cannot change what happened a minute ago, but you can determine what happens in the next by making that choice to get up again. And once you have settled it in your mind that there is a tomorrow after today, you are ready to begin again. Life will at times present us with harrowing surprises. There will be disappointments even when are genuinely doing good and in pursuit of our dreams, and how we overcome will be determined by what we do with what has happened to us. So after everything you've lived through, resolve that you will not live a life any less than an extraordinary one. Take everything that has happened to you and use it as a driving force to rewrite and rescript your life.

As l reflect on the things that were built from the courage to start over, I realise the power of the human spirit that surfaces when we think we have reached the end. Today I stand on my feet with the utmost humility as an award-winning author, business owner and an Academy for women entrepreneurs' graduate. All those beautiful changes only came after l made the decision to get up again and dream again. Had I forfeited the courage to start over as unbearable as it was, I am not so sure I would have evolved into the woman I am today.

I bear the scars of the things I survived but they are only there to remind me and those watching my journey that it is possible to overcome the valley. That is why I wrote this book for me and every other person who needs assurance that a new beginning is possible.

"Show me someone who still has breath in them, and I'll show you someone who still has a chance."

YOU CAN BEGIN AGAIN...

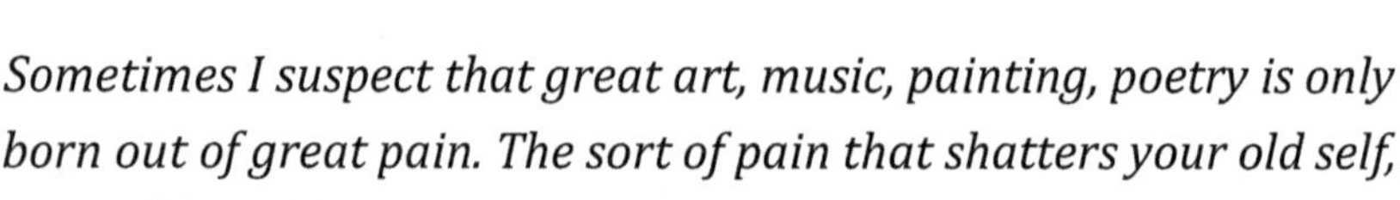

Sometimes I suspect that great art, music, painting, poetry is only born out of great pain. The sort of pain that shatters your old self, your old world-view and compels you to give birth to a new one...

Harold Kushner

Chapter 1

BROKEN DREAMS

A tree is considered "lifeless" when it bears no fruit. "Lifeless," that is the perfect caption to have described my life in the season my dreams collapsed at my feet. The very things that I felt had begun to bring fulfillment and meaning to my life, seemed as though they were being stripped away from me, one after the other. My purpose was on the line and my hope and the very belief that certain good things were within reach slowly began to fade away.

For one, 1 could not figure how I had gotten here. In my mind, 1 was on a path 1 desired and what 1 perceived the One above was leading me to. I was a young woman with dreams trying to change her narrative when tragedy struck. Like every other dreamer 1 had packed my bags heading to a completely different continent in an effort to build a better life, not only for me but for everyone who would benefit from my stability and progress. I needed more than I had and the relocation made perfect sense for me as a writer. It was also part of my poverty escape plan from a country that has crushed a mountain of dreams for so many. I even imagined my name someday making it onto the New York times best seller list but that dream soon became wishful thinking.

In chasing that opportunity, I was unprepared for the disappointments and rejection that sometimes follow when you are in pursuit of your dreams. The dreams 1 carried soon turned into broken dreams, crushing into a pile of rubble at my feet. I pretty much wrote off that year, that's how deep the dark hole 1 was in measured. Being back at the very place 1 was trying to escape was heavy on me. A place where running water has become a luxury not a necessity. An economy so stifled that it gives people no time to dream because they are either looking for water or queuing for money. Long queues at the bank resemble ones you would find of people waiting to enter a concert; always ridiculously long. An ailing healthcare system that has stolen life and basic human rights from the vulnerable. A place where the bare minimum has become exclusive to the elite. Having to contend with my new environment proved to be the ultimate test of my strength and resilience.

Dejected as to why every door of opportunity refused to open for me in a better land, I probed the Creator of the Universe for answers. Was it the colour of my skin? I kept getting so many Nos even in instances 1 believed it should have been a Yes. There seemed to be no fair chances for someone of my hue. Or could it have been that it just wasn't time? I mean I watched others win; so was it just a lash of terrible luck? But God was silent...

The worst state of confusion is when you're walking in purpose, submission and transparency yet your life is the worst it's ever been. I should have been in a season of harvest for all the good seeds 1 has sown, my life should have been at its peak, but here was something threatening to bury me. In that moment if you would have told me that God doesn't know my name, I would have believed you. It was as if 1 did not exist in his database, and it always seemed He chose the hardest battles for me.

You could mistake my life for a fictional movie because I seemed to go through the oddest things. Who goes from an American dream chance to mediocrity and water woes? You would think that somebody is secretly filming my life because the upheaval I was experiencing, is only the kind you see on TV. My life looked nothing like what God promised it would be. I was a dreamer with an empty reality. My life mortified me. I felt so lost and confused. I could no longer tell the front from the back because life seemed to be pulling me in every direction. I lost my vision and could not see anymore.

That particular year turned out to be a very grim one for me. When everything in my life should have been unfolding the way I had hoped, the opposite was happening. My reality was in forceful conflict with my dreams. Everything that could have possibly gone wrong did and even turned out worse than I imagined. I couldn't believe that something like that was happening to me. I was in the midst of a raging storm that did not seem to be subsiding but was rather getting stronger by the day.

I suddenly felt cheated by life. I had a once in a lifetime opportunity to progress and build a meaningful life, and that chance could have changed my life forever but; it yielded nothing. During the day I would put up a strong front, but at night time it was Niagara Falls unleashed. I felt robbed of my dreams, peace and happiness. In that season I was stripped of my identity, I was lost and blinded.

So here l was asking God; why me? When will my fortune change? I questioned God. I questioned my purpose and everything l thought was true. It's not expected that life should be rainbows and ponies, but it should be meaningful. I was burnt by life chasing shadows, something l knew I would never catch. I watched my efforts yield nothing and it brought me to my knees. These are the kind of things that are hard to come back from.

There is nothing as piercing as unrealized dreams and unfilled expectations. You see l had spent the last years just getting by, but with a new found purpose I now had a deeper sense and meaning of life, but that was now being threatened. After having gone through the whirlwind emotions of trying to understand why all that was happening to me, I also had to start asking myself the real questions. What do 1 have left? Who do 1 have left? How can 1 begin again?

And that is how the journey of remembering who I am and coming to myself began.

I am the master of my new beginning.

I remembered that my life was authored before 1 was born. I was reminded that God's plans for me are for good and never to harm me.

I had to regrasp the fact that 1 was born with an infilling and the world needs what 1 am carrying. I took control of my life and finally understood that 1 am the master of my new beginning. So understand this, as the battles rages on, God knows the plans he has for you. His plan still stands when you are in the furnace.

Maybe things were great for you at some point, but along the way you slipped. Maybe you were hurt or the chances you took ended up on lost street and you began to doubt your very existence. The view of yourself changed, doubt creeped in, then blurred lines...

Maybe there were times in your life when thoughts of the future exhilarated you and there were no limitations in your dreaming. In the primitive of your innocence anything was possible and getting out of bed was pure excitement but, somewhere along the line something in you died along with your dreams. In such moments you have to begin to realize that you can create new dreams. In it all, never forget that before you were born, your life was already written.

If ever you forget or need to be reminded of who you truly are, look into the word of God. It is your mirror and true reflection of self. Let it strengthen you and be your source of confidence. Circumstances often make us forget who we really are, but never let experiences taint what you know and believe is true.

Life will at times present you with overwhelming warfare, things that seem too great to overcome. Those harrowing surprises where you find yourself at the forefront of a battle where the enemy is vying for your destiny. Secret battles that threaten to wreck and derail your purpose. I know what it's like to wake up and be stripped of everything you ever believed in. To have your hope snatched. To wake up and not know if you are going to make it. To lose something treasured. To be too wounded to speak, too wounded to pray or get up. I still don't know why certain things had to happen to me, but l can't deny the growth that came through it. I am all raggedy but I've grown. I'm in tatters but I'm changed.

And so I've settled it in my mind that; after trauma, divorce, heartbreak, a tragic loss, bankruptcy, disability or an event that left you questioning humanity, you can start over and rebuild. There is a life to be lived in fullness after tragedy. So, always summon up who you were before the cares of life got the best of you. You can still build a meaningful life out of broken dreams.

Broken dreams should not be the end, you can begin again.

------- ··◆ ❦ ◆·· -------

The caterpillar does not die in order to become a butterfly, it simply transforms. That is the perfect illustration of coming to yourself, your real self.

------- ··◆ ❦ ◆·· -------

CHAPTER 2

COMING TO YOURSELF

Some call it a tale or parable, but a story is told of a carefree young man who demanded that his Father give him his portion of inheritance so he could set out on a journey of independence. Being the free-spirited person that he was, he squandered his inheritance in a flash and soon found himself homeless in a faraway land. He went from being the most eligible bachelor in town, fast cars and a life of revelry; to filth and repulsion.

It is hard to overlook his irresponsible choices, but what 1 find most fascinating about this story is what happens to him in the moment where life has battered him senseless and he is so hungry that he is feeding with pigs. It is said that in a turn of destiny, "he came to himself." Let's pause for a minute. This way of life could have carried on for your years, he could have tried to build comfort around his circumstance and even died in that foreign land but the story says, "he came to his senses." I would like to believe that was the very moment where he became "unshackled." Something on the inside of him was prompted and he began to realise that he was more than this and was meant for better. So he got up with a new sense of hope that he still had a chance, and not only that, but a new found character of humility and dignity. It is fair to say that the misfortune that he encountered was one he had created for himself but he rose above it. If there be any value in this story of the prodigal son is that we should approach God with the mentality of; "my Father can still do something for me."

There is a "coming to yourself" that takes precedence in the transformation story of your life because that is where your turn of destiny begins.

Life challenges often weigh at our hearts and bout our senses. They batter us so hard at times that we forget who we are. There is a coming to yourself that takes precedence in the transformation story of your life because that is where your turn of destiny begins. Where you get up and say surely this can't be it! Where you refuse for the narrative to remain the same. A place in your mind where you trump to believe that you can never be free, you can never be fruitful or do great things.

There are moments 1 have had to remind myself of who 1 am, that I still have purpose and 1 can begin again. This stands true for you too. You have purpose and you can begin again. After everything you've lived through, resolve that you will not live a life any less than an extraordinary one. The caterpillar does not die in order to become a butterfly, it simply transforms. That is the perfect depiction of coming to yourself, your real self.

You can begin again.

We stumble when we look back, the future deserves a chance. You can still build a meaningful life out of broken dreams.

CHAPTER 3

CREATING NEW DREAMS

The day 1 launched my own publishing house was a dreamlike moment for me. The last time 1 had reported for work was two years prior, and this is not because 1 never chased opportunities, but for the strange reason that the doors 1 kept beating on just wouldn't open. I seemed to be dealing with what 1 term, "the almost syndrome." I almost secured a permanent position at a large corporation, 1 almost settled in America, 1 almost established myself; 1 almost got a breakthrough.

Every time 1 put one foot in the door, 1 would be pushed back out. And so 1 flew halfway across the world just to move back in with my mother. Sigh...broken dreams and rock bottom. Thirty-three years old, broke and unemployed. I always seemed to end up right where 1 began. When 1 would meet friends and family 1 would dread the question; "so what are you doing these days?"

In response I would try to be most confident and say, "I'm still focusing on writing books." And 1 would often be met with, "what about work?" Sigh...dry seasons and dead ends.

Could it be that work just wasn't for me because God desired that 1 enlarge my capacity to be a business owner? Realizing that 1 might soon become a liability 1 sat down and began to reflect. I looked within so 1 could start with what 1 had. What strengths and skills did 1 carry? I am an author so how can 1 perfect my skills and create something meaningful? Apart from my writing 1 had been editing and proofreading books for other authors for over a year. People would also approach me to review and endorse their books. So 1 began to enhance my skills by also teaching people how to write books. I soon realized that many had confidence in my abilities, so why not publish books for them?

And so, my journey of being a publisher began. Many witnessed the beautiful moment but they missed the tears, the many times I've been written off and told 1 contribute nothing. The prayers and restless nights as 1 tried to pick myself up from the ashes. I did the time...

I never gave up because 1 created new dreams out of broken dreams. I sat down and wrote ones greater than those that had failed, I realized that 1 could begin again. When you don't know what to do with your broken dreams, create new ones. Take everything that has happened to you and use it as a driving force to rewrite and rescript your life.

We are often afraid of creating new dreams because we fear that they will end up on the same dusty shelf of unrealized ones. A part of me did not want to write again but here 1 am penning yet another life changing book. I was frustrated in my purpose, but 1 had to go back to the real reason why 1 started, and it is that the world needs my books. If you ever feel frustrated, always go back to the reason why you started. Purpose will always supersede fear. No matter how you feel, the world needs what you are carrying. And if you ever feel exempted from that truth, it just means you haven't tapped into your purpose yet.

If I had forsaken the courage to begin again, my publishing house would not exist and I wouldn't be telling great transformational stories written by other

Fear is deceptive, hold on to courage.

remarkable authors. Sometimes I think fear is a false image appearing real because we worry about things that have not happened and may never do. Fear is deceptive, hold on to courage. You can still build a meaningful life out of broken dreams.

The most important thing a man can choose is how he thinks...

Marcus Aurelius

CHAPTER 4

PUT ON A NEW MIND

The story of Phiona Mutetsi is one that which for the first time, 1 heard of a game where one can discover a new way of thinking, as well as wholly lose their fear. When she played chess, she says she was never afraid and knew she could win. So great was her story that it was turned into a best-selling book and a highly esteemed movie where she got to be called the "Queen of Katwe." A girl who grew up in the slums of rural Uganda turned into a global marvel for adopting the principles of chess into her real life.

The principles of chess are said to teach people how to think deeply about their decisions and also challenge one's intellectual capacity amongst other things. But, if

I could to put it my own way, I would say chess teaches one to navigate through life from a position of strength and better understanding. It redresses your mind and gives you a healthier insight. It is true that we all won't play chess but we can adopt its principles in our regular lives.

Watching one of her interviews 1 could see her radiate so much confidence and self-belief through the screens as she said these words:

"Hope wins in everything you are doing. It's up to you to wake up, stand and then do something. You have to plan; you have to strategize and also, you have to have dreams."

A typical morning dress up routine should be considered incomplete without putting on a new mind.

All this got me pondering on the certainty that, a typical morning dress up routine should be considered incomplete without putting on a new mind.

Understanding that notion soon makes you realize that you have been thinking the same way for years. Putting on a new mind is not some motivational gibberish that life coaches teach, but it is rather a biblical principle that precedes any change or transformation that happens in one's life.

Isn't it amazing that out of all the human anatomy and make up, God said to renew your mind in order to see transformation? My life changed the day 1 understood how much power 1 possess in having the ability to choose my own thoughts. To know that 1 may not be able to choose how 1 feel, but 1 can choose what my mind focuses on. After shattered dreams, painful ordeals or failure, 1 can make that choice to put on a new mind and begin again.

Your clean slate doesn't start at the beginning of a new year. It starts when you put on a new mind and begin to change the way you think. I can make all the resolutions 1 want, but as long as 1 move into a new day or year with the same mindset and way of thinking; nothing changes. There is no new you without a new mind. You can't begin again without a mind redress. New dreams will require a new mind.

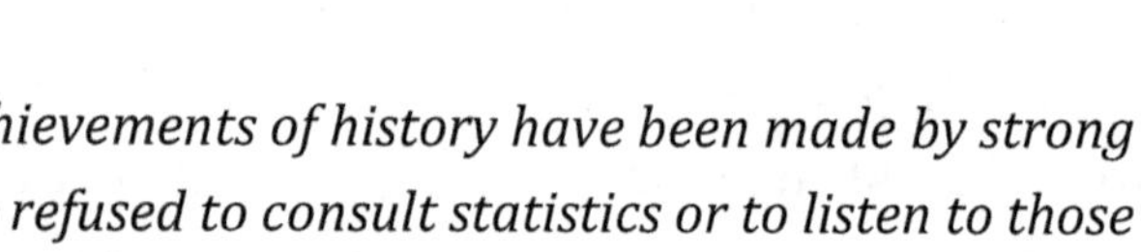

All the great achievements of history have been made by strong individuals who refused to consult statistics or to listen to those who could prove convincingly that what they wanted to do was completely impossible...

Eric Butterworth

CHAPTER 5

LEAVE ROOM FOR POSSIBILITY

About two years ago 1 got an opportunity to travel to the United States and it is there that 1 met a lady who took an interest in my first book "Why 1 never gave up." She would always go on about how she sees me associating with great people and would often say, "girl 1 see you sitting down with Oprah, she loves books." One unusual morning she sat across a table from me and with the highest confidence said; "you should write a letter to Donald Trump." Ok what?

First of all, I am an African. Secondly, we all know how he feels about people from African countries. But 1 said all that internally. Without really asking me how 1 felt about it, she went on to write the Whitehouse address on a piece of paper and gave it to me. What I found amusing is the fact that she truly believed the President of the United States would read my letter.

This was strange and beautiful to me because l had never met anybody who thinks so highly of me and believed in me more that l did myself. And so l did, yes l wrote a letter to Donald Trump and expressed how l felt l could be of value to the American society through my writing and how important my content was in addressing mental health issues because my book was an echo of hope.

So somewhere in the oval office possibly lies a letter from this black author. Whether it was tossed or filed that doesn't matter. What matters is what that experience taught me. That wonderful lady challenged me to see life from an angle l never thought imaginable. She literally unshackled my mind from timidity and inferiority. She helped me gain so much self confidence that I have begun to see no opportunity as beyond my league. My mind just doesn't think the same or in limits anymore even if l tried.

I found myself pondering on this question recently; "why did that lady see possibility where somebody else could have seen disappointment?" It is because she has a mentality that refuses to conform to the norms. She was audacious enough to believe that the President of an influential country could read my letter as crazy as that sounded. Her chances were nine in ten and that is the way we should view things if we are to be unleashed.

Life will require you to be an independent minded individual, a non-conformist or better said a maverick. We adapt but never conform.

Get to a place where you learn not to conform to the status quo or what the world deems as realism. In relationships, business or whatever endeavors you take on, be an independent-minded person.

One of the greatest writers of all time taught me to never center my dreams around an ailing economy, what the newspaper says or what the stock market depicts. He taught me that my dreams should always be independent of external factors. If my inner wealth is well defined, 1 can live a full life in the emptiest of places. Life will require you to be an independent minded individual, a non-conformist or better said a maverick. We adapt but never conform.

The originator of the philosophy, "leave room for disappointment" likely killed a lot of dreams. People began to do life walking on eggshells with such an anxious mind of, "anything could go wrong at any time." In business, relationships and careers it ignited a fear of things that have not even happened yet and may never do. How does one succeed in anything when their mental state is always anticipating the worst-case scenario? There is a renewing of the mind that needs to charge in at some point in our lives because of the misguided notions we were taught. I choose to leave room for possibility.

In every circumstance look for and leave room for possibility. You can begin again.

EXERCISE

I believe in tackling life encounters in a practical manner, so I came up with an idea of listing what I call my "LEAVING ROOM FOR POSSIBILITY GOALS" to help create an internal atmosphere of positivity in a world filled with so much uncertainty. I would love to challenge you to do the same no matter how unattainable you may think they are. Listing goals is a way of keeping your hope and courage alive. The will to pursue your goals becomes more real when written down.

So go ahead and list your five ***possibility goals.**" As an example, you can list them as:

1. To get my driver's license by June 2021
2. To buy my first car by November 2021
3. To start my first business by January 2022
4. To complete my bachelor's degree by 2023
5. To make a deposit for my first house by 2024

Whatever it is you would love to see come to fruition, write it down. You will need a clearly inscribed vision to be able to begin again.

I have embraced more people now than I ever would have with two arms...

Bethany Hamilton

CHAPTER 6

FINDING PURPOSE IN ADVERSITY

In the year 2003 a young budding surfer went for a swim with a friend. Whilst looking out for tidal waves to ride on, a shark reeled up on her and bit her arm of. With her friends and family in deep fright, she was rushed to the emergency room in a pool of blood and shattered dreams whilst fighting to live. Without warning, her life changed forever. She could kiss those championship trophies goodbye. Those unruffled whiles of both arms stretched out whilst balancing on her board were over. But in a complete change of destiny, she returned to the waters and went on to win her first national title, and because of her captivating courage, her story was adapted into a movie. Not long after, she was inducted into the surfer's hall of fame and became an author and philanthropist. After such a painful tragedy, Bethany Hamilton realized that she could begin again and still live a full and meaningful life. She accepted her new condition but did not let it determine what she could become. When asked how she could possibly see the good out of such a tragedy, her response was; "I have embraced and served more people with one arm than 1 would have with two." She found purpose in adversity and you can too.

People beginning again start to see something greater than their pain and losses. They see something extraordinary coming out of their tragedies. If you could just allow yourself to see beyond the things that broke you; you can begin again. There are people whose lives will never be the same because of their tragedy. Somebody has to learn to walk again, live again and dream again. And that is when the human spirit subconsciously fights for what is true and conquers. Refuse to come out with nothing.

What do we do with our pain so that it becomes meaningful and not pointless empty suffering? If this happened to me what do I do now?...

Harold Kushner

CHAPTER 7

SHOULD WE ACCEPT THE BAD THINGS THAT HAVE HAPPENED TO US?

When Harold Kushner wrote the book "when bad things happen to good people," he says he knew he would write a book for those who wanted to go on believing, but whose anger at God made it hard for them to hold on to their faith. His three-year-old son was diagnosed with a degenerative disease and would only live to be fourteen. It is then that his outlook shifted to asking the question; *"what do we do with our pain so that it becomes meaningful and not pointless empty suffering?"*

There are some things and life experiences that are difficult to understand and the question we often direct to that is; "why did it have to happen to me?" That divorce, that cancer, that business that failed to take off, that futile engagement. I believe 1 am not the only one who has ever felt that they did not get a fair chance at something. That the miracle we were hoping for did not come at the time we really needed it. We ask those questions but no matter how much you wish you could go back to yesterday, you can't. It's unfortunate that the past cannot be changed, but it does not mean the future is fated either.

Acceptance is acknowledging our current state so we can begin to deal with it and heal from it.

Accepting the unpleasant things we have experienced is not agreeing with what happened, but it is us saying; "1 can't do anything about yesterday, but 1 can do something about tomorrow." Acceptance is acknowledging our current state so we can begin to deal with it and heal from it.

We don't always choose our circumstances and experiences, but we have the ability to choose who we become from them. Give your pain a voice. When you use your pain for good, you are giving it a voice of hope for others trying to survive what you already have.

Your tragedy is your work of service; because you lost a child you now know how to counsel grieving parents. Because you lost everything you are smarter and wiser to teach others about financial literacy. Because you went without for so long, you now know how to show compassion and love in "deeds." Maybe you grew up without parents and it has taught you how to look out for the orphans because you know what it's like to need someone but have no one. You take the things that broke you and use them as a means to help others.

It is often hard to accept things we cannot change but doing so helps us move forward and begin again. You can begin again.

Affirmation: *"My past is over; l am letting go of what did not work. I am alert and l am present, my tomorrow is greater than my yesterday. I can begin again."*

God the healer will heal the damage to our faith that was created each time we prayed and saw no results...

Glaphre

CHAPTER 8

GOD HAS WRONGED ME

I had never questioned life in so much depth till the day I sat reflecting on my life and it looked like I had never uttered a single word of prayer in my entire existence on this earth. I have never at any point expected my life to be perfect, but looking at the way it was in that particular season, you would swear I had never whispered an honest plea. My life looked like a tidal wave had hovered over it leaving a disastrous scene. It looked like a sorry site.

You would think that my life would reflect the God in me, but it was nothing short of empty. I had tried to play the strong woman for so long yet my life was in shambles. In that period of my life I had stopped running from my Maker and had made a commitment to honour him. I was praying, serving and walking in obedience yet behind the wall I stood face to face with the reality of what my life really was; "empty and broken." I had seeds in the ground but harvest hadn't come in season and I had nothing to show for it except the breath in my lungs. Behind the walls I was the struggling Christian, the broke one, the one battling things nobody could see and the unemployed one.

I couldn't remember the last time I had not lived on my toes. It was battle after battle, one trial after another. When do 1 get to breathe? I would sigh. I hadn't had rest in years, and I'm not relating about going to bed at eight in the evening and waking up at six in the morning. I'm talking about inner peace that lasts for more than twenty-four hours before something is wrong again. I was washed-out...

I remember how pathetic 1 looked as 1 begged for a chance and opportunities to turn my life around. For the first time in my life 1 felt like God had wronged me. It was as though he had turned his back on me. It was those kinds of moments when you know you need a miracle more than any other person in the room, but it doesn't materialize. Was God unjust, I mused? If He is not unjust why does he then permit bad things to happen to good people when He could have stopped it? I was suddenly becoming such an angry person because of what life had done to me. In that place I did not feel like I was learning, instead I felt as though I was losing myself. I wasn't running from the will of God when I ran into distress, I could not say I was here because I made a foolish decision. I wasn't winking at sin.

Then the many questions started. Why me? Why was this happening to me? How could I have stopped this from happening?

We ask so many questions because we want to understand our pain; why is this happening to me? The first phase is denial, then reality hits that this is actually happening. Then follows rage and anger. The wrath of, "1 prayed but 1 did not get the job. I fought so hard but I still lost the opportunity. I fought so hard but I still lost the one I love."

Then bitterness why me? At least to my understanding, an earthly father would rush to their child's rescue but God seemed to let it play out. I will not even pretend it did not hurt; I won't pretend 1 wasn't entertaining the thought of interrogating God. I felt God had broken my heart. Now 1 understand what Job meant when he said; "God has wronged me."

Through the questions and criticisms of God, a wave of truth suddenly hit me that, God hurts when we hurt. He doesn't take pleasure in our pain. In that moment it felt like 1 was wearing God's heart and could feel his compassion for me. I somehow had found new eyes to view certain things from.

If God is not unjust, then maybe He's misunderstood.

And so, I have concluded that if God is not unjust, then maybe He's misunderstood. If the things 1 go through don't change who He is, then maybe 1 should change the way 1 see Him and my circumstances.

A broken man who could not reconcile his reality with the promises of God asked him this unriveting question; *"Lord if you are truly with us, why has all this happened to us?"* Instead of telling him why, God directed him on what to do next. He told him to go on and move forward with the little strength that he had left. In other words, he was saying; *let go of the past. Let go of everything that failed. Let go of every disappointment because you will still have to walk into tomorrow.* What happened ensued, and it is not every time that we will find closure. As hard as it is to accept, there are certain things that cannot be undone.

Acceptance is a healer. Understanding that yesterday will never come again gives us the courage to face tomorrow.

CHAPTER 9

WHERE WAS GOD?

A man who had just lost his son stood up to share his ordeal during a church service. From the tremor in his voice, you could tell he had been crying and was still in a broken state. He says he asked God, "Lord where were you when my son died?" And God answered; "I was right where 1 was when My Son died." Surely the man who created heaven and earth could have stopped his own son from being hung on the cross. But He did not for a greater purpose that many could not understand at the time.

Looking back over my life, my struggle with God was with the things he allowed to happen yet possessing the power to prevent them. Have you ever found yourself in a place where you feel as if you are making excuses for God? Almost like you have to justify Him to yourself as to why everything failed. A place where you are so angry that prayer seems like a mockery. A place where the war always seems far from over. A place where you are even afraid to pray again because of the losses and failures you still experienced when you prayed the first time.

In my personal battles I have had hard questions for God too, and l needed answers. In that particular season I write about, like Job l could not understand my pain. I just could not make sense of the fiery trial. I felt abandoned by God and embittered by life because I truly believed I did not deserve to suffer that way.

And so I asked; where was God? At that point it wasn't rage, it was a daughter's heart questioning her Father why he would allow her to hurt this way when He is God over all. I didn't want God to treat me like a soldier or somebody made out of granite and that nothing could break me. I had feelings and I was human. In that moment I needed Him to be a Father and not God. But my reality at the time made me feel like l was claiming a Father who did not even know my name. Almost like l had given God a role that he did not want to fulfil. I was seeking answers about life and felt like God owed me an explanation.

We often feel indifferent about God in our pain because we know him to be able to do anything. So when he permits things that leave us gagging for life, we feel betrayed because we believe he could have stopped it. When God permits very painful experiences, they don't leave us questioning if he's powerful, but whether He is just. I never at any point concluded that there is no God, I just began to assume that he was so unjust.

If He didn't cause it, why did he allow it to happen? Perhaps you often say to yourself, but if he had come through maybe 1 wouldn't have lost the child, 1 wouldn't have been divorced, 1 would have gotten the visa, I wouldn't have lost everything. At times you even begin to think you would you do a better job at being God? Those are the nerving thoughts that play over and over in our minds when we are going through something hard.

Although I have had trust issues with God in the past created by moments where 1 felt he let me down, I still believe that He can take the most tragic of events of our lives and turn them into something that can change the world. It happened but it wasn't all for nothing. When I grew through my experiences, I also began to realize that I've been so angry at God over circumstances where somebody practiced freewill. It was a person that hurt me. It was a person that segregated me. It was a person who treated me unfairly and denied me a fair chance. It was a person who broke my heart. It was a person who made me lose faith in humanity. I had misdirected anger.

Not everyone will choose to do the right thing. Somebody made a choice and 1 suffered heavily for it, that's how powerful freewill is. If God always twisted the arm of everyone, freewill would not exist. He would just impose himself on every person which is not in his character or nature. Those who compromise your destiny are people trying to play God with your life. God is not the enemy.

When you're in this world you will face some kind of trial no matter how good of person you are. But through it all, you do not have to tread alone. You can learn to trust God again and begin again.

Begin to look at the challenges in your life as something that can be fixed and overcome.

CHAPTER 10

DEALING WITH REGRET

God in his superiority once experienced great regret. When he realized that the people he had created were not these cosmic mellow creatures, it is said that his heart was filled with so much regret. I can only imagine God with his hand over his drooping head thinking; "what have 1 done?" I'm sure the "what ifs" and "if only" questions began to swirl intensely in his mind in that moment.

"He was sorry that he had ever made them and put them on the earth. He was so filled with regret that he said, "I will wipe out these people I have created, and also the animals and birds, because I am sorry that I made any of them." ... But the Lord was pleased with Noah.
[Genesis 6 vs 6-7

But because he is God, he turned out to have a redemption plan for his regret. But then again, he wouldn't be God if he did not have one, right?

Sinking in regret is exactly how some seasons of life often feel like for us human beings. We go over the regrets of the chances and risks we took but are not paying off, the good things we did that don't seem to be yielding anything. The prayers we prayed that came back unanswered, and the litanies that came to naught. We begin to see everything as a waste. Why did we pray if we were going to lose in the end? We look at our shattered hopes and dreams that have been reduced to a mole of sand and wonder if we will ever recover.

As hard as it is to come to terms with certain realities, I believe that the recovery plan God had for His regret, will be the redemption that will lift your life from the pit. God put a big "BUT" after his regrets. "But I can still fix this because of one good man Noah." Going forward begin to put a "BUT" in any life circumstances you may find yourself in.

"But I can recover, but I can heal, but I can love again, but I can build a new business, but I can begin again."

Begin to look at the challenges in your life as something that can be fixed and overcome.

There is a way that God can take your past and mistakes, and fit them into His eternal plan for your life. He totally flips the script and uses what was supposed to tear you down to instead elevate you. He is the spring that shoots you up when you've reached the very low of rock bottom.

FROM BENEATH TO THE TOP

A little girl from Sussex London could have never imagined the life she was yet walk in when she was born. Growing up with a speech impediment, she was constantly teased and bullied. As if she had not gone through enough, this once little girl became a woman, got married but eventually divorced. With life evidently not getting any better, she started living on welfare cheques.

Looking like the epitome of failure she took to writing but her manuscript was rejected by twelve publishing houses. But refusing to stay at the feet of failure, she braved on until her first book was finally published by Bloomsbury Children's Books. Her 4th book went on to sell three million copies in its first forty-eight hours. Her 6th book did even better selling nine million copies in twenty-four hours. Her 7th book broke records becoming the fastest selling book of all time reaching a staggering eleven million copies on its first day. Already basking in the glory of great success, her books were adapted into films which have grossed in over seven billion dollars worldwide. I share this story to remind you that, you have a chance just like the little Sussex girl.

I know you may think you are beneath consideration, but never let those who may have a flawed revelation of you determine what you can become.

AND NOW I WILL

There have been many times in my life where I have found myself swimming in a sea of regret. Unintelligent choices, walking blindly and mis stepping have made me fall more times than I have ever picked up a dime. But as I evolved and grew, I realized that I can do something about certain things I did not get right the first time around by introducing the rule of; "and now I will." Part of my change was centered around my money habits and gaining financial freedom, and it began with me adopting the mantra, "and now I will."

"Now l will make better financial decisions and budget more. Now l will not get into anything blindly. Now l will plan ahead and use caution. Now I will do better."

All this was not said pretentiously, I took it seriously and followed through with actions especially when it came to saving money. For the first time in years I had a significant amount of savings when the year began and it gave me so much peace and flexibility in my day to day carry-ons.

If you ever find yourself saying: "I wish I had done that, said that, been that, pursued that, experienced that, then now you will need to learn to follow it up with; "and now 1 will." You won't always be able to go back and fix the past, but you can adopt the rule of; "and now 1 will."

It's better to do the right thing now than to spend a lifetime trying to undo and fix all the things you did not do right.

Rewrite your dreams as if everything were possible...

CHAPTER 11

DEALING WITH FAILURE

Most mornings I wake up to a notification on my phone that says; "temperature is over fifteen degrees, adjust outfit accordingly." At times I am even prompted to grab a jacket or an umbrella on a cloudy day. It's almost as if there is a phone amoretto guiding me, cautioning me and, mentally and physically preparing me for my day. The sad realism though is that life doesn't often work that way. There is no proceed with caution banner for life's most untold events. Natural life does not always come with such warnings, we pretty much live through each day hoping and striving for the best.

In reality you never really wake up to a phone angel telling you that everything as you know it to be is going to change, so get ready. Life doesn't tell you that today you will get disappointed so prepare your heart emotionally. It does not tell you that you should not take that business risk because you will lose everything. It doesn't tell you that you will lose a loved one.

Life rarely gives warnings, the way it usually happens is that we get unexpected distressing surprises. Nobody can accurately predict "every" event that you will experience in your life apart from the Creator, and failure is one of those things that no one fully prepares for.

Nobody in this life ever plans to fail. No one ever exerts effort with a vision to yield nothing. When we plan and pursue our dreams and desires, it is always with the goal to succeed. Regrettably, plans do not always turn out the way we hoped or imagined. There are often unforeseen circumstances that we then have to confront and overcome, one of them being "failure."

I hate to fail, even though it's something that has happened to me a number of times. It was the spring of 2019 when I was convinced by somebody to have a second book launch for my first paperback in my home country. I considered this particular individual a friend and respected and trusted their judgement as 1 had seen him excel in his own career. At the time of our discussion I had a sense of doubt and did not really have the desire to have a second launch but his convincing pitch made it hard for me to say no. "Are you sure it will work?" I implored. "Off course it will" he responded, which was followed by a power point presentation of why it was a great move for my writing career. So I went ahead and took the plunge.

The organizing process seemed so easy which was a rather enjoyable surprise and the high-ranking speakers l reached out to as well were more than willing to support me. I printed flyers and made a clamor about it on social media. My brother who has been one of my greatest supports got my books printed for me in South Africa and they arrived in my country right on time. All this coming together is what I took as a sign that I will have an amazing book launch. I was expectant. However, on the day of the launch is when l would learn that likes on social media do not translate into actual support. It started with the friend who brought up the idea not showing up for me. Another person who had initiated and asked me to get a bigger venue (*silly me I did*) did not show up for me. The instrumentalists who were supposed to play that night stopped taking my calls.

I was hurt and flustered. As I was processing all the emotions, I still had to get up and speak. I promised myself I wasn't going to snivel in front of my parents, so I waited till 1 got home to deal with the burden on my heart. What baffled me is that the prominent guest speakers with full diaries showed up for me, whereas people 1 considered my village left me in a lurch. It was heartbreaking. Had it not been for my phenomenal MC and other wonderful guests and friends, I would have crumbled. The event later turned out so beautiful but when it was all over, the questions remained. Did he give me that idea so he could see me fail? What could I have done differently to have avoided this?

When dealing with this failure I learnt that I should never do something against my conscience, subsequently I have since found several other ways to deal with failure which I share below.

SEVERAL WAYS ONE CAN DEAL WITH FAILURE

- **Draw hope from those who have achieved that which you desire.** Jack Canfield the author of

"Chicken soup for the soul" was rejected 144 times before his book was published. When one publisher decided to give him a chance, he was given a royalty check for a staggering one million dollars. Today his book has more than a hundred million copies in print.

- **Use caution** and plan diligently in whatever you do or pursue.

- **Don't be afraid to believe again.** If belief were a feeling, I think none of us would get up and do anything because we feel fear, we feel doubt, we feel worry, we feel tired and we feel pain. But you have got to hold on to faith more than reason and our feelings.

- **Rewrite your dreams as if everything were possible.** I love the story told by Napoleon Hill of how he cut out the word "impossible" from his dictionary. His undisputed success is a witness to what happens when we believe. Your expectations can be exceeded.

- **Don't put limits** on who you can become because of what happened a minute ago. Keep evolving.

- **Never rule out possibility.** I have learnt not to rule out possibility because 1 have seen extraordinary things happen for so many people. Who told Barack Obama that he could be the first black President of the United States? Dreamers are fully convinced of their dreams before they share them with the world. Likewise, be fully persuaded of your dreams, when your self-resolve is strong, nothing will deter you.

- **Do not be afraid** of the future, you can write the one you desire to see.

- **There are certain things in life that should be refused.** Shame can't be all you know. Stagnation can't be all you know. Cycles can't be all you know.

- **Understand that greatness takes time.** Good success is progressive.

- **Share your life lessons from your falls.** We are often afraid to share our truth because it reveals a part of what makes us feel shame where we should actually feel courage because we survived.

For many, that place of failure seems so familiar because they have been there so many times. You seem to always be at a beginning when you should have been progressing and possessing. Failure and disappointments make you afraid of the world. You feel afraid to go into the real world and make friends, pursue goals or attempt anything because you are afraid something will go wrong.

Because of fear, we often walk around with untapped capacity and potential. Our gifts and abilities sometimes lay dormant waiting to be put to use, and until we rise above fear, we may never discover what we carry. He who discovers the treasure within, is one who exploits the reserve.

Don't ever for a second think that courageous people never feel fear. They've just learnt mental composure in the most unsettling circumstances. One of the people 1 look up to once said to me; "1 don't mind failing, if 1 try something and it doesn't work, I'll try something else." After failure is always time to rebuild and try again.

What would you do if you weren't afraid of anything? What would you fight for? What would you dare to pursue? I'm grateful to those who have gone ahead of me and achieved the impossible, because of them, I can now be brave.

It is easy to lose yourself in the valley because it is often a dark place of despair, but prayer can help us survive the valley.

CHAPTER 12

ARE YOU HURTING? PRAY

Being an aunt means I get to baby sit at times when I visit family. I get to be one who breaks up the petty squabbles, cradle the crying ones and play mentor to the young ones. During one of my visits to the sweltering city of Windhoek in Namibia, I was tasked to look after three kiddies all below the age of ten. As routine, after all chores were done, they got time to play. One afternoon during playtime I heard bickering and quarrelling in the next room.

Just as I was getting up on my feet to go check what the fuss was all about, I heard my niece say to her brothers, "I will look up to heaven and pray" in her screaky distraught voice. I just smiled because her innocence and trust that there is someone up in heaven who could fix everything really warmed my heart.

The innocence of a child is like water, so pure and honest. From time to time we need to adopt a childlike approach to life's challenges. We need to *look up to heaven and pray*. The scripture that encourages one to pray when they are hurting was etched in the word of God because, when you cry out to God, he sends help. It doesn't matter if you created the circumstance or you fell.

Look up to heaven and pray.

HANDLING THE VALLEY EMOTIONS

It is a natural instinct for people to want to know what to do when they are frustrated, when they are depressed, and when they don't understand and question God. When going through immense hardships, your emotions become like a yoyo, always going UP and DOWN. Broken dreams, frustrations, anger, discouragement, discontentment, feelings of failure and stagnation soon become the norm and make your heart sick. Dealing with valley emotions is often us trying to make sense of our pain but never truly understand it. Like why we have to hurt so much before we can heal. Why we have to endure before we breakthrough, and why we find ourselves in the valley sometimes.

It is easy to lose yourself in the valley because it is often a dark place of despair. A place where you can spell your name but don't know who you are. Prayer can help us survive the valley. When you pray, it is one place where you cannot hide your heart from God. You know he won't laugh at you or shake his head at your misery; he won't see you as weak, but sees your brokenness as a sacrifice. That's the only place you can be vulnerable without judgement, so look up to heaven and pray.

IN THE WAITING, PRAY

The waiting season is so difficult. You even feel as though you'd do a better job at being God. You begin to feel as if he's taking too long or he's not rightfully handling things the way you feel they should be. The season of waiting calls for crazy faith and prayer of thanksgiving for that which you are waiting on. It calls for believing in something greater than your reality. God answers prayer, but we cannot choose the way he does it. So, in the waiting we trust and give thanks.

Gratitude is liberating. You lose that sense of entitlement and begin to realize that you seemingly have so much more to be grateful for.

CHAPTER 13

PRACTICE GRATITUDE

If there's one area of my life that 1 have often struggled with, it's gratitude. The struggle is not with people but more toward God because it always seems hard to be thankful when things are not going right. But that soon changed for me.

As an active social media user 1 love to take on communal media challenges that 1 feel will help me grow. In this instance 1 decided to try a ten-day gratitude challenge that was shared on a ladies group that I am a part of. We were to list ten things we are grateful for, for ten consecutive days. When 1 began this challenge, it was out of a pure heart to learn because 1 struggled with gratitude toward God, especially in moments when 1 didn't understand something or did not have enough. I remember lettering this down as my prayer:

"Lord 1 struggle with gratitude, especially when 1 don't have enough. In moments when nothing is going right, it's hard for me to say thank you. I would love to learn about gratitude. Please teach me dear Lord my heart is open."

After that prayer my gratitude practice began. This is what 1 would script and audibly say out.

- I am truly grateful for the gift of life. It means each day that 1 wake up, 1 get a chance to begin again.

- I am thankful for possibilities.

After just drafting two sentences, I took a pause and plainly wrote, "getting to ten seems hard." I was faced with a genuine struggle of trying to find what 1 could thank God for. But when 1 began to recount daily events that changed my life, 1 realized how 1 seemed to have so much to be thankful for. So 1 continued…

- I am grateful for warm clothes, a warm bed and warm blankets.

- I am truly grateful for the tonsil removal surgery 1 had, really needed it.

- I am grateful for my writing ability.

By the time 1 got to number ten so many emotions had stirred up in me and 1 was crying. It was a moment of realizing that familiarity had made me overlook so many things 1 was to be always thankful for. And then strange wonderful happenings started flowing in.

On day four 1 woke up to delightful things happening all around me, including a six-year debt being completely cleared. I would like to believe it was the posture of my heart that started creating miracles for me. That particular day had begun with surprise calls and messages from people just wanting to bless me financially. It had been quite a challenging month for me as 1 had just starting my publishing company and had only clocked one client.

As a beautiful surprise, my dad called me to say he wanted to meet up and buy me groceries, and give me money as well. Whilst meeting with him a lady who had promised to purchase a copy of my first book sent a message to confirm that she had sent the money. Still celebrating a wonderful start to the day, somebody 1 had not spoken to in years sent a message to say he had deposited money and directed me where 1 was to pick it up. Wait a minute, how was all this happening in one day?

The last message was a shocker because I had a nightmare of a history with that person which left me in debt and on the verge of being blacklisted. It all started years ago when 1 wasn't quite emotionally sound and made so many crude decisions that make me cringe when I think about them. I often say we are all a little intelligent until it comes to love. It's still a mystery to me how we seem to lose a bit of our intellectual capacity when we find somebody to call love and all the platitude pet names.

When I met this man, it was through a mutual friend and I really did not think we would build a relationship. But then started the giggles at the bell notification of an incoming message. The holding of hands for the first time and the cute blushes from being told you are beautiful. Total bliss...it's always beautiful in the beginning. Months passed with this man, and even in moments where there was so much toxicity in the relationship, we seemed to paddle on with our feet in a boat that was guaranteed to sink and overturn. I called it love and building with your man. As someone who had a bit more financial flexibility than him and was driving, he often borrowed my car to run errands or go out with his friends. One fateful day he asked to use my car to go view a place he said he had always wanted to take me to. I thought, "oh how charming and thoughtful of him." I truly believed he wanted to celebrate our love by taking me to a place I'd never been to before. My naiveite appalled me sometimes.

In good faith I gave him the car, and when it was time to pick me up from work, l received a call and on the other end of the line was a man in panic mode. Rushing through his words as if he was being chased, he kept saying I should come to the accident scene because he crashed the car. At first l thought it was a prank and he was just testing me, so my initial response was, "you are lying." But when he continued to say, "no look I'm serious" I soon realized that this was no joke. Not wanting to sound inconsiderate, I asked if he was ok and he said he was alright but was just a little shaken. Turning to one of my close colleagues, I explained what was going on and asked her to drive me to the scene. When I got there all I could say was "no no no" and gust out a loud cry. In all my years, that was the first time I had cried that way. Onlookers who were passing by must have assumed that someone had died because I was wailing and there was no comforting me. I wept for hours; the car that was only three weeks old looked like it had just been pulled out of the scrapyard. I had sacrificed so much to be able to buy a fairly new car, but it had all come to nothing.

The weeks that followed were hell, you would think out of a good conscience that man would help me to get the car fixed, but instead he ghosted me. Pictures of him with his ex on his profile soon surfaced. So whilst I was sinking into debt and nursing a broken heart, he was playing happy family with someone else. He did not give me a single dime to help me out, so I dealt with every blow on my own to a point where 1 could no longer sustain myself with my salary.

For years I struggled to pay off the bank and the debt accumulated from trying to fix the car till they started sending letters threatening to take legal action and blacklist me. That is when you begin to see that there is a very thin line between love and hate. The hate I developed for him almost consumed me. I could not understand how a human being could treat somebody else with the utmost contempt and disregard.

I had lost a lot in my lifetime but this one left a sting in my pocket. Each time 1 would think about my car and look at the reality that 1 am now a pedestrian my heart would break all over again. How could 1 give my car to a man who hadn't even put a ring on my finger? I loathed my gullibility. I invested so much and walked away with nothing but a bleeding heart, and I remained paying for something 1 no longer had. It would be six years before we could have civil conversation.

After so many years of us not speaking, I decided to reach out to him and explain that I could no longer carry the burden on my own. It was now time for him to take responsibility for an unideal circumstance he left me in. It was affecting my career and personal life as 1 could not progress with that six-year debt hanging over my head. The goal was to be debt free and not necessarily gain closure because a part of me didn't want or need it from him anymore. I had completely healed from my past.

Some things will take years to recover from, and it's not because you will be thinking about them every day but for the reason that to fully come to that place of healing, you need time. It took years for me to get to that place of complete healing.

To my surprise, when I finally did speak to him, he acknowledged how irresponsible and immature he had been in the past and was willing to clear the balance owed to the bank. He promised to send the money in about two weeks and I was just to wait for his confirmation. For some reason, I had no expectations after he said that.

The week that we spoke happened to be the one where I had starting practicing gratitude, and so I went about my life without any high hopes that he would deliver on his promise. Shockingly, in less that twenty-four hours of us talking he had sent the money to clear the debt. I was astounded, what was it about gratitude that unlocks such blessings? It's as if at every turn people just wanted to bless me. For the first time in six years, I found a deep sense of peace. The weight of debt was lifted off my shoulders and I was finally free. This was one of those things 1 never thought 1 could recover from, but by day five of practicing gratitude, I was debt free. God assures us that he will give us double blessings for all our woes. The restitution should be two-fold for every single thing we went through and 1 was receiving mine.

Why is gratitude important? Gratitude is liberating. It is freeing in the sense that you begin to realise that you seemingly have so much more to be grateful for. I lost that sense of entitlement and finally understood the principle of gratitude. Gratitude is also an energy that unlocks blessings that were being held up.

Furthermore, gratitude is not just about thanking God for what he's already done, but it's also thanking him for what he's about to do. My personal thanksgiving went something like this:

- Yahweh, for every wonderful thing you're about to do in my life thank you.
- For every door you are opening, thank you.
- For meeting every need, thank you.
- For every breakthrough, thank you.

The true test of faith though is practicing gratitude when you are in chains, when you are in a dark place and have nothing. But when you begin to thank God for his promises that seem like wishful thinking, you soon understand that, in that moment you are declaring and invoking the power of God in your circumstance which brings about peace and makes you less anxious. The moment you are liberated you will realize that your gratitude released something.

Practicing gratitude helps you deal with really hard realities. It shifts your mind and attitude from the factual and what may be horribly wrong in that moment, right onto the immutable power of God.

Allow God to bring to your mind times when He has helped you. Make note of them... Glaphre

CHAPTER 14

FINDING YOURSELF

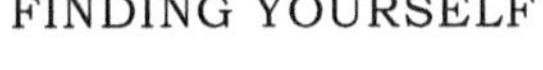

Not so long, a young lady reached out to me on social media on a page I run named after my first book, "Why I never gave up." Quoting her words, she said to me; "I still wanna know more, like why you never gave up." In essence what she was asking is; "so what changed?"

What changed is that I finally found myself and discovered the real reason why I was created and put here on earth. Purpose was my saving grace and it gave me the will and strength to get up again. I did have self-doubt in the beginning because I did not feel qualified enough to take on those things pre-ordained for me. Questions such as, "who am I to write books" lingered on in my mind. But God whispered, "the world needs yours books." So I got up, trumped all my fears and chose to be courageous in my new found Purpose. The one who gives you Purpose, is the one who gives you ability and qualifies you. So you may not know what it is yet, but the world needs what you are carrying.

Not knowing your purpose is a hard-hitting thing. You will try so many things some which you were never meant to attempt all in an effort to find yourself. So, what then does it take for one to discover purpose earlier in life so they do not wander? These are some of the self-introspection questions that have helped me greatly.

- What do you find easier to do that others may find a little difficult?
- What strengths do you possess that people praise you about?
- What are you passionate about?
- If you could serve the world what would you want to share with it?
- What do you love to do? Even when you're tired you find yourself wanting to push on.
- What gets you excited?
- What do you look forward to when you wake up?
- What gives you peace when you do it? What gives you a sense of therapy?

- What is that one thing that has helped you and could possibly help another?
- What gives you confidence when you think about the future?
- What have you overcome? What have you found a solution to?

Always remember, you were already in the mind of God before you walked a day on this earth. You were a thought; you were a purpose, and you were a vision of God. The highest calling or purpose of any human being is to serve. As you find yourself, look for how you can serve because purpose is when your resources, time and money have served another.

So, find your identity. What happened to you or may be a part of your story should never suffice as a true representation of who you are. You are more than the total sum of your experiences.

BELIEVE IN YOURSELF

James Allen the author of the world-renowned book, "As a man thinketh" did not want it published. Being the perfectionist that he was, he felt it was too shortcoming and not worthy of print, but his wife Lilly Allen convinced him to have it published . At twenty-one pages, a book described as small enough to fit into your pocket soon became his most famous one and made him a household name. How many times have we talked ourselves out of our dreams because we reckon they are too insignificant or not good enough? Going forward believe in yourself, what you despise the most could bring you into your greatest prominence. It's enough.

---·◆·❧·◆·---

And when you do start over, make your dreams even bigger.

---·◆·❧·◆·---

Chapter 15

YOU'VE GOT TO BELIEVE IN SOMETHING AGAIN

Have you ever been so disappointed by life to a point where your will to move forward is taken from you? Where absolutely nothing makes sense and you have become another statistic just getting by? In some moments, life will leave us no option but to begin again because that may be the only way to regain our lives after trials and detours. After every setback, hardships or mishaps you have to believe in something again, you have to start over and grow your wings with each step as you try again. I know life got hard and almost destroyed you but whatever you can find that can make you believe again, seize it and hold onto it.

Find encouragement from what other people have overcome, draw inspiration from a TV programme or a motivational podcast. It could be a book or a short video clip from YouTube, whatever you can find that make you believe again, embrace it. And when you do start over, make your dreams even bigger. Write down the things you desire to achieve when the storm has passed. You won't always be in the gale, the sun will shine again.

Build your strength and watch the way you speak to yourself when going through something hard. I know at times emotions can be screaming; "listen to me!" But you've got to challenge your thoughts and accustom yourself to not finishing a negative sentence in your mind. Building your strength sums up the words of encouragement you whisper to yourself day and night till they are reinforced and imprinted in your heart and mind.

Also remember, before you possess you have to see it with invisible sight. It means you are not using natural sight but insight or internal perception. It is possible to have perfectly good sight but a blind mind, so sometimes you are not tripping on stones but rather mental blocks. I've begun to realise that, starting over and pursuing great things will require you to believe in the impossible. It will implore you to put aside all logical reasoning and walk by invisible sight. To have a certain conviction about things that are still to manifest. Faith has sight; invisible sight.

WHAT DO I DO ABOUT TODAY?

A couple of years ago in my most broken state 1 asked God an honest question. My life felt like such a sham and I couldn't quite understand my environment and everything that was happening around me. I couldn't make sense of anything that didn't seem right at the time and I couldn't understand why my life was stagnant. So seeing that he is this great heroic who can do anything as seen by all the good associated with his name, I asked him how was 1 to get through the now? Yes the promise is for tomorrow but today still demands that I live through it. So what do I do about today?

When my heart is aching and my life is in the rubble, what did he expect me to do? When 1 can see there is nothing for dinner, and moments when I'm confused. Times where I have the vision but no reality. Moments where the world is blaring; it will never happen for you! What do 1 do?

God then made me grasp the truth that, in seasons where I may have to wait, is where I should practice gratitude towards him for every single thing I am trusting him for. In waiting seasons, you prepare for that which you are hoping for by thanking God for it every day till you clutch it in your hands.

SO l JUST FORGET IT HAPPENED?

It's often the emotions that come with remembering where you've been that can make your scars bleed again. Letting go of the past is not developing permanent loss of memory. It is rather releasing it so you do not miss that which is ahead. Maybe we dwell on the past because we haven't seen our restitution. To make up for the past we need something new to console us, but the new will come when we begin to make room for it by releasing what's behind from our hearts.

GET UP

A woman fed up of constantly being beaten by her husband decided to enroll for self-defense classes. She began to build her strength and developed a level of resistance against attacks. One night the husband came home and taunted her wanting to do what he was habituated to. To beat her black and blue but was clueless that his wife had been learning to fight back. Wanting to punch her in the face he missed and received a blow himself. In shock he looked at her with that, "did you just punch me in the face glare?" She was done taking it all laying on the ground. She was done accepting that life. The enemy gets surprised too when we start fighting back. When we refuse to accept things that are not normal, we are fighting back. When we refuse to accept stagnation and refuse to accept cycles, we are fighting for our freedom. Determination is needed to win, refuse to accept things that God did not preordain for your life. Get up and fight with the little strength you have left.

*No, do not go home and punch your husband in the face, this story was for exemplification purposes only. *

YOUR MENTAL CAPITAL

One of the greatest lessons 1 have learnt is that your mind is capital too. I was enlightened on this when a woman who was sharing sound advice on starting businesses mentioned that people often say they do not have money to start their business but forget they that their minds are capital too. So, what are you doing to enlarge your mental capacity? What are you adopting to help you believe again and broaden your aptitude to receive greater? You see, there is no physical wealth without mental wealth. Likewise, there is no new beginning without a mental one.

THE VISION BOARD

The world around you won't always agree with the ideal life you have built in your mind. With aggression you will feel the need to give in but, you've got to fight to hold on. A vision board gives you substance and a mental picture to hold on to so your dreams don't die within you. Sometimes called a dream board, it is described as a collection of your desires in the form pictures as well as words of affirmation. When all that is pasted and put together, it helps keep your hope alive when your reality is tugging hard at you to give up. When 1 made my first vision board, 1 cut out pictures and words that aligned with my ultimate goals out of magazines, and WING UP Publishing was one of them. Today it stands as a fully functioning company that started off on a vision board.

You need to create an internal environment and economy. It is what will sustain you in the wilderness. How do you create that environment? You do so by creating a vision board, speaking the future you want to see manifest, as well as reading books and the life changing word of God. You can also consider refining or learning a new skill so that when the sun finally shines you are ready to meet your opportunity right at the break of dawn.

THE POWER OF WRITING THE VISION DOWN

Most of the good things that have happened for me were written down way before they ever manifested. It's almost as if when l write, I birth the unseen. As one call things that do not exist into being, I script them into being. In doing so, the power l carry to turn the page and begin again becomes evident.

You and l possess the power to redesign our lives and it often begins with writing the vision of your desires down. Some things don't seem so powerful until they are written down.

So write the vision down.

THE REFINING OF YOUR INNER DISPOSITION

Back in the nineties when I was in Junior school, I had a run in with the headmistress; her name was Miss Kats.

She was a sweet but firm lady who loved to wear pink cardigans and pulling socks and for some reason, I got on her wrong side. I can't vividly remember what I had done wrong, but she was so upset with me that she summoned me to her office and told me I was going to be punished. I was never a rebellious child and to hear her say that made me want to sob, but I kept it together as I awaited my fate.

She then said to me as punishment I was to master Psalms 27 and she would not let me off the hook until I could recite it in my sleep. What in the world? What kind of punishment was that? To recite a whole bible scripture? I mean that was unheard of. When a teacher ever punished students, it was mostly blows to the fingers with a duster or filling in four blank pages with the sentence, "I will never make noise in class again." And you would write until your hand is cramping and sore. So her form of discipline was new to me and I thought wow, she must really hate me to give me such a sporadic punishment. All I knew from the bible was; "for God so loved the world" the famed John 3 vs 16.

She gave me a bible with the old testament and there I was in the boarding school hall reciting, "the Lord is my light and my salvation" day after day. I would go to her and roll off my progress but she would send me back if I missed a verse. At the time I thought it was torture but I had no idea she was plating seeds in me. You would have thought being forced to read the bible would make me so bitter and resentful towards it but the thing is, the word of God is so pure and washes like water. When I thought I was being punished, I was actually being washed.

I carried that scripture in me for years and little did I know that it was my covering in moments I had no one but God to look out for me. There are things I've survived that I shouldn't have. But God...

Sometimes you are not being punished, you are being refined for your new beginning.

FACE TO FACE WITH YOUR INNER DISPOSITION

An innocent man who was falsely imprisoned wrote a riveting statement from prison. It read, "they have me in chains but they can't touch my mind." That declaration was a very powerful revelation in showing us that, challenges can physically weigh us down but they can't braze our minds if we begin to understand the power we possess in having the ability to choose what our minds focus on in adversity. Our priced possessions are our minds because we can create new conditions by using the power of insight where we begin to look for possibility within before without. The value in that is in discovering hidden treasure we never fathomed we carried because great things happen from the inside. How often do we hear people say, "1 didn't know who 1 was until 1 was put in a situation where 1 was forced to grow. I didn't know 1 had it in me" when they take on a challenge that yields success. There are certain seasons which reveal who we truthfully are, as well as some of what we need to improve or change. That is the moment you come face to face with your inner disposition, uprooting everything that doesn't make you better and replacing it with everything that helps you grow. I believe that everybody has the capacity to transform.

Being face to face with your inner disposition is also gaining mastery over your mind when the world around you doesn't make sense. It is being resolute and summoning your courage when you feel fear, and proclaiming your breakthrough when absolutely nothing is working. That is how you begin again.

CHAPTER 16

PREPARE FOR NEW OPPORTUNITIES

Once upon a time in the year 2005 I was one such person consumed by the love of music and could not go a day without singing. As a high school student in a boarding house, I had a routine whereby after supper before study time I would sneak into a free class or the school hall and belt out songs. It was my place of comfort and solace.

One particular day whilst rehearsing, one of the teachers happened to pass by and heard me singing. He walked in on me and here I was thinking, boy oh boy am I in trouble for using the school hall without permission. He went on to ask who I was and relayed how he was drawn in by my melodic voice. I introduced myself and let him know that it was a custom for me to rehearse at the school hall if it was free. He commended my commitment to music and told me he was the school choir director and desires to see me grow to fruition because he felt I had such a wonderful gift.

He soon signed me up for a singing competition at a prestigious arts theatre to perform. Because of that I began to develop a sense of inadequacy but he instilled so much confidence in me and assured me that I had what it took to win. I went on to the competition accompanied by a few friends who were senior prefects. And there I was, an eighteen-year-old me taking on my first hefty responsibility. Backstage I was so nervous that I made sure I registered to sing last in the category of musicians because I needed so much time to pull myself together. Never had I been that anxious in my life.

When my turn to sing finally came there was no more stalling. I had come face to face with my fears. I got onto the stage and sang the popular song, "How do I live" by Liane Rimes. That sigh of relief when I was done was such a warm appeasing feeling.

Then came the results announcement, I recall there being a girl who played the guitar, she really stood out and seemed to be the biggest threat. In my mind she sure was the winner. As everybody waited in anticipation nerves and all, I was called out as the winner. SHOCKER!

I was dazed at how it was even possible that I could win such an accolade, it left me in such wonder. I was so happy but could not even show too much emotion because I was awe struck. My win soon made news at school and one odd assembly day the headmaster decided to honour me and a few other students in their respective accomplishments. Nobody was told in advance so it's something I wasn't aware of. As a senior in high school I had days where I bunked assembly (something I'm not proud of) but as seniors we just had this notion that it was boring and unfashionable. When the headmaster began to call out names mine was one of the first but I was nowhere to be seen.

After assembly as I left my dormitory heading for class, one of my friends came up to me almost in a panic saying my name was called out in honour of my competition win and no one could find me. I was so shaken because missing assembly could have serious consequences. I immediately rushed to the office all apologetic and had to come up with a reason why I wasn't in attendance. Fortunately, I was still given my gift.

I was reminded of this experience and it made me realize that, it is very easy to miss out on great moments and opportunities because of passivity that our gifts are going unnoticed. It also made me think deeply about how many opportunities we forfeit because of unpreparedness when fortune comes knocking on our doors.

Do not miss out on an opportunity or your day of honour because it found you not ready. Master your craft and skills and gather as much knowledge on your field as you can. And always be in a state of readiness, you never know who's watching.

We don't always choose our circumstances and experiences, but we have the ability to choose who we become out of them. What are you doing with what has happened to you?

CHAPTER 17

YOU HAVE THE POWER TO CHOOSE

After any experience we go through, we always come out different people. But who we come out as on the other side of crisis will be determined by what we do in the now. How we process every emotion and how we challenge and control our frame of mind. We don't always choose our circumstances and experiences, but we have the ability to choose who we become out of them.

What are you doing with what has happened to you? Every circumstance is waiting for a response or reaction from you. Worry, doubt, fear, anger? Which will you choose to dwell on? Your experiences may have deeply hurt you but what are you morphing into? You have the power to decide. You can pick yourself up and build from what you have left. You may ask, but what do 1 have left? Life; and because you have it, it means you still have a chance. Who do you have left? Do right by them and honour them.

You are not responsible for the way your journey begins, but you are responsible for the way it ends. You are accountable for what happens next; your choices, the time you take to think, the way you plan and your commitment to being a better person.

The world is turbulent but as we grow we learn to be resolute in the storm. Finding peace in the storm is having surety that God will bring you out. And as the world evolves, we all have the ability to become who we need to be.

We fall, we learn, we get up, we begin again.

Sometimes the environment won't be kind to your vision. Your faith will demand that you stretch it so that resistance and geography do not limit your dreams. Getting something you've never had, will require faith you've never had...

CHAPTER 18

STRETCH YOUR FAITH WHEN YOU MEET RESISTANCE

THE WOMAN WHO REFUSED FOR HER FAITH TO FAIL

There once lived a woman who could never stop bleeding and in time it earned her the tag, "the woman with the issue of blood." When I think about this woman, I picture someone in an extreme state of physical and mental burn out. A woman who had become an outcast in her community because of an ailment that seemed irremediable and bizarre. I see a woman who was thought to be the curse of the neighborhood, no friends or companionship, and the kind that you make room for with your nose covered when she crosses your path.

I can only imagine the labels they had put on her; "the stenchy one, the one not marriable." The mockery and taunts she endured day by day must have been so much torture to her already pale and fragile frame from bleeding ceaselessly for twelve years. She was somebody who had spent her life savings and probably sold everything she owned just to find a solution from the world's greatest physicians for an issue that her ripped her to shreds. She was a woman who had travelled city to city to find relief and even if would have been just for a few hours or days, she was ready to take it. Just a minute of peace would have been a gift to her soul, but there was not a single thing anybody could do for her.

For twelve whole years in distress, the most reputable doctors and specialists in the world could do nothing for her, but instead left her in a worse state than they found her in. Could there have been a more broken person than her? Bankrupt, suicidal, depressed and crying herself to sleep every lone night. But one fateful morning a good Samaritan knocks on her door and asks, "have you heard about a man named Jesus? He's in town." When 1 read this story one thing 1 kept asking myself was, "what would make her hope that this time it just might be different?" She didn't know this man; it was all based on hearsay that he could perform miracles. What prompted her to get out of bed and take that one last leap of faith? I mean years of damage to her body must have left her frail and weak. Where did that strength come from to disregard the pain and walk by faith? What made her want to try again when her failures were more in number than her birth years? Was she not tired? Why did she not pray for her own death? Had she become some type of prisoner of hope?

When she finally got to Jesus it is said that she thought to herself, "if only 1 could touch the hem of his garment 1 shall be healed." For some time I've been trying to make sense out of this. On the outside it looked like she was wasting away, but on the inside she kept her hope alive by what she kept saying within herself; "*1 shall be healed, 1 shall be healed, 1 shall be healed.*" And she was completely healed and cleansed.

This incredible story helped me understand that, 1 may face resistance whilst trying to get to my destiny, but what 1 keep saying within myself is what will help me break free to breakthrough. What are my repeated thought patterns when I am convinced I've reached the end? Faith is fight, 1 will have to strengthen my feeble knees, get up again and fight till 1 overcome. My desire for change and to be free has to be greater than my tiredness. When you know that you don't want to carry that burden anymore you will stretch your faith like the woman with the issue of blood. She refused to defer her hope. The distance between you and the promise is faith.

PRACTICE FAITH BY A SPOKEN WORD

A few years ago, 1 got a hold of the book, "Oprah the biography" and something caught my eye as 1 perused through the pages. It is said that before all the fame and fortune she would audibly say:

"I'm destined for great things, I'm going to be huge, I'm gonna be on TV and people are gonna like and know me. I think I'm really gonna be kind of famous, my mandate is to win."

And bam! Years down the line she became the world's first black billionaire. This got me thinking long and hard. Could it really be that everything starts with a spoken word? And as you do so, your words set in motion certain things like resources, the right people suddenly being brought along your path and even getting rare opportunities presented to you. It's almost as if the universe literally connives to align and make your words a reality. She started speaking from invisibility, to create what she could see. She created the seen from the unseen just as God created the earth from what was not visible. Our words are invisible but we use them to create what we can then see.

You cannot just dream and think it, you've got to speak it. Even God in creation had to be audible, therefore faith requires confession. A new beginning will necessitate that you speak it into existence. It will require that you speak what you desire to see. When God said we should call things that do not exist as though they did, he was opening our eyes to the truth that we are co-creators and that there is so much power in our words. We have the authority and dominance over our new beginnings. We are in a strong position because of the power of our words.

Sometimes the environment won't be kind to your vision. Your faith will demand that you stretch it so that resistance and geography do not limit your dreams. Getting something you've never had, will require faith you've never had. Resistance should be met with stretched faith. Every time 1 find myself in the deep pit of adversity, getting out always seems to be predetermined by faith. In one such a season, 1 made a conscious decision that as hard as it was, 1 was going to stretch my faith. Stretching is uncomfortable because it pulls you out of your comfort zone and you soon learn to disregard the now and hold on to the promise. I called myself an entrepreneur before 1 was ever one, claiming things that were not even in my hands yet but today I have them.

So when my eyes tell me my situation can never change, 1 stretch my faith. In crisis 1 stretch my faith. When you're practicing faith, there is always something trying to make you reason out everything. A tussle between logic and revelation. When they say, "faith is fight" it is a showdown between logic and a promise from God. Reason versus truth. But the latter holds more strength.

In practicing faith, you also learn patience. And I'm not talking about waiting in a long queue at the grocery store without fuming; I'm relating to learning patience in the sense that, you learn to endure whilst sustaining your faith. You hold on without letting your faith slip away. What is faith?

Faith is addressing the present as though the better future has arrived. Addressing today as if it's already tomorrow. Addressing the current as if it's the greater latter. Faith is your moving forward substance. You can begin again.

CHAPTER 19

THE BLIND CHEF

*"I'm living proof that dreams come true against all odds." ...
Christine Ha*

Christine Ha shocked the world by becoming the first blind winner of the esteemed cooking show MasterChef earning her the name, "the blind chef." She wasn't born blind but gradually began to lose her eyesight due to a condition called neuromyelitis Optica.

It is a tragedy to come into this world with fully functioning eyesight but only to lose it at a later stage. This young charismatic woman had plans for all the great things she wanted to achieve, but that detour almost killed all her dreams. After losing her sight, Christine had to relearn so many things so she could adjust and live her life differently from what she was accustomed. The freedom to do everything independently was taken away from her without anybody ever explaining to her why it had to happen, and why it had to be her. But through it all, she refused to give up on the life she believed she could still live even after the loss of her sight. She started to dream again and cook again. With a few adjustments to her daily routine, she found a way to navigate through life with her new condition. Christine Ha only won the world's biggest cooking title because she built the courage to begin again. Her misfortune became her blessing and opened doors for her that were only ever a dream at some point. By starting to dream again, you are giving the future a chance. If you never give anything a chance, you may never get to experience certain things. Your desires are within reach, but sometimes you just need to stretch yourself a little.

TIIME AND CHANCE HAPPEN ARE FOR EVERYONE

The race is not to the swift, nor the battle to the strong, nor bread to the wise, nor riches to men of understanding, nor favour to men of skill; but time and chance happen to them all...Ecclesiastes 9 vs 11

When I first read the story of Esther Mahlangu I was completely blown away. If you do not know who this powerhouse is, allow me to enlighten you. Esther Mahlangu was born in 1935 in Middleburg South Africa. She is a woman who has never set foot in a school, but became a global icon for her Ndebele paintings and artwork. So great was her talent that she was approached by BMW to devise an art car for the BWW 525i.

You most certainly have to be on such a great level of success if you have your cultural paintings being adopted as a design for one of the most lustrous car brands in the world. Not only that, her artwork was also used on some of the British Airways fleet. Esther was further conferred a doctorate and today that woman who has never been to school is addressed as Doctor Mahlangu. And that is how time and chance happen for all. Never do yourself an injustice by thinking certain great things are for a select few. Time and chance are for everyone.

CATERPILLAR TO BUTTERFLY

If nothing ever changed, there would be no such things as butterflies...Wendy Mass

There was a time in my life I thought I would never amount to anything. You see the typical African dream for a woman is for her to graduate from University, get a good job, never get pregnant out of wedlock and when all that is in place; she then settles down. Mine was pretty much a fumbled dream.

Teenage mother, single mother, changing diapers whilst others are bagging their university degrees. I had amassed all the accolades of failure, especially the one of "least likely to succeed." The shame, the brokenness, the labels, the stereotype, the rejection, being written off completely; I thought I had reached the end. I genuinely believed that this was the best life could do for me and so I just went with it feeling my way through life. However, discovering my purpose was a defining moment for me. It is when 1 realized that the chances I was never given could still happen for me, and that the last could be first. That is why I liken my transformation to that of a caterpillar morphing into a butterfly.

The transformation of the caterpillar to a butterfly has been called miraculous and is depicted as the perfect metaphor for change. It too fascinated me so much that I set out to study its evolution process. As part of its progression, it goes through the cocoon phase which I call the secret place. This is the development stage where it sheds off what's unnecessary and builds its strength, thereafter emerging as this beautiful winged creature. What I also found inspiring is the fact that caterpillars are designed to be butterflies from birth. A caterpillar is born with a purpose to become a butterfly. I would like to believe that human beings are also born with a design to be great, and detours and trials do not change that. Don't die in your cocoon when you are destined to be a butterfly.

Out of God's most beautiful created creatures, my favourite has surely become the butterfly. You see this thing first emerges as a slimy hideous creature everybody wants to trample on and walk past. But when it evolves into its dazzling beauty, everybody begins to chase after it just to catch a glimpse of its magnificence. Its reproach soon becomes its prominence. I know you may think you are beneath consideration because of the season you are in but give time; time. You will grow into your power. The people that wrote you off and walked past you, will soon be chasing after you. How do you explain a thing whose body rests on the ground suddenly having the ability to soar? It is just awe inspiring and mind-blowing. That is why I believe butterflies were created to remind us of what's possible.

Don't hold a tin cup under the Niagara of God's plenty...

Eric Butterworth

CHAPTER 20

ASK FOR THE MOON

THE BREAKTHROUGH PRAYER

In my lifetime 1 have prayed countless prayers, but the most compelling one 1 have ever prayed is one that is known as "the prayer of Jabez" in the bible. Jabez was a man born of immense sorrow such that his mother gave him a name that best matched the pain he had brought to her.

Although he grew up to be an honorable man, there were certain events in his life that he could not make sense of. I would like to believe that he was a moral and upright man who did everything by the book, but for whatever reason, he had nothing to show for it. He was still living in limitation, lack and in nothingness. An honorable man prays and gives to his community, surely Jabez must have fulfilled all those things to be given the title of being "honorable." But after having done all those things, nothing in his life was changing or yielding much. Was it his name that had tied him to chains because it is translated as, "one who makes sorrowful?" Was his name now affiliating him with unpleasant experiences? This man seemed to be dealing with something that the world could not understand. He was a man carrying a desperation to be set free from every chain and weight that kept pulling him down. Life had seized to be a gift; it had no meaning. So in a moment of desperation, this man prayed:

"Oh that you would bless me indeed and enlarge my territory. Let your hand be with me, and keep me from harm so that I will be free from pain." And God granted him his request.

Any man who begins a prayer with such a deep groan of "oh" has suffered and passed through a lot. Jabez's prayer carried intense emotion that expressed the desperation to finally see his breakthrough. I understand his prayer as somebody saying to God...

"I'm looking for something I've never had. I've been in the shadows too long. I don't know what my purpose is. I'm tired of being reduced to nothing. I'm tired of being in lack. I'm tired of being broke. I own nothing to my name, please give me land. I desire more than the ordinary. I want to be free from the tragedy that is associated with my name. I want to be free from pain. I've been through enough, Lord it's far too gone, please give me rest. Please give me a new beginning."

This kind of prayer was enough to move the heart of God such that He heard and granted him his request. It was riddled with honest and pure emotion, a daring and bold prayer. Jabez realized that if he did not pray differently, he would live a long but empty life. He thought to himself, *"surely if there is a God in heaven, he can change my story and I don't have to continue living in emptiness.'*

As I studied more about this prayer and why it carried so much power it dawned on me that this plea is a deliverance prayer. It is a prayer that liberates from chains, recurring cycles, generational curses, failure and things we cannot see with the naked eye. It unshackles you from your past, broken dreams or anything that may have never worked. After that revelation 1 sought to take on the 30-day Prayer of Jabez challenge that was popularized by Bruce Wilkinson who wrote a book after its name. When 1 began to say that prayer from the very depths of my heart 1 started to sense that 1 was being unshackled from something. Even my sleeping pattern changed and my nights just became more peaceful. I also started getting so many creative ideas about business leading to the launch of my publishing house.

Each time 1 discover something that changes my own life, 1 always can't wait to share it with the world so other people can be transformed too. If you are reading this book, 1 would like to challenge you to start doing the prayer of Jabez for the next thirty days. There is a power and an unshackling that comes from this prayer.

Whatever circumstance you might be faced with, find the will, courage and strength to pray this unusual prayer that brings unexplainable blessings and breakthroughs. Jabez was asking for restitution for all he had been through because at times the only compensation we need is a massive breakthrough. God granted his request, yours should be next.

UNSHACKLED

Have you ever found yourself in a place where you've done your absolute best but it yielded nothing? Where everything you try finds its way back to your feet? Where failure has become the norm?

When we've lived through life in the same chains, similar cycles and unchanging circumstances, we begin to strongly desire change and to find a place of rest in our struggles. In flashes when today constantly looks like yesterday and tomorrow promises to deliver the same, our souls begin to war for something different. When dealing with the identical pain, frustrations, failures, broken relationships and issues we start to become so unsettled about being caught up in the same cycle of things. A bottomless longing takes a hold of our souls to be "unshackled." To break free from whatever is keeping us from our destiny, so we can break through. And so we begin to ask ourselves; what will it take for me to be free? What will it take to be successful? What will it take to see real change in my life? How can 1 break free from everything that has me in chains? How can 1 significantly change my narrative? How can 1 be "unshackled?" How can 1 get a hold of something I've never had?

When you begin to ponder on those questions, it signifies that you are ready for a transition. That uneasiness that makes you want to leap up and act is a sign that you are ready to be unshackled and transformed so you can begin to live a meaningful life. A life of bondage that is full of pain and struggles is one we should refuse to get accustomed to. Now lies the even more important question that many ask; where do 1 begin? Yes, I have established that 1 need an absolute change but where does being unshackled or unbridled begin?

Being unshackled often begins with desire. Desire will fuel your dreams and cause you to be unshackled. Because you want to be free you will get up and try something you never have. You will begin to introduce new things into your life that can help you grow. Because you desire generational wealth, you will get up and pursue something different no matter how fearsome it is. I love the story about the richest man in Babylon. When the leader asked him how he got to be the wealthiest man in the land, he expressed that it all began with a desire. What is your desire?

In my penning this book my hope and desire is that 1 shed light on what it takes to break free. It is my desire to see you the reader break free from mental and physical barriers and see a solid and complete change in your life. A part of me believes that you did not just pick up this book but you made an appointment with destiny.

There is one gift your troubles cannot touch; your destiny....

Max Lucado

CHAPTER 21

YOU CAN'T KILL DESTINY

In the year 2010 whilst on a night shift, four men walked into my work place as regular customers would. As per the norm at this restaurant, we the waiters would stand by the entrance to welcome guests and sit them down. On that particular day I happened to be the one standing closest to the door and here l was with a huge smile on my face thinking I will be cashing in big on tips that evening from these four gentlemen who seemed they were all there for a good hearty meal. "Good evening; table for four?" I asked.

With a grin the leader slightly nodded his head and like a bolt from the blue, he pulled out a gun. In a panic my colleague who was standing next to me quickly emptied all her pockets and gave them her phone and all her tips for the night before they even asked for anything. The leader then grabbed my arm and directed me to walk to the till so he could empty it out. When a man has a gun and is waving it around like a trigger-happy chap you simply comply, so there was no screaming or shrugging on my part. I did not know this man and how much of a conscience he either had or did not have, so I just did as he asked. When we got to the till, 1 explained to him that it was locked and we had to get the keys from the cashier who was seated a few tables away. He then forcibly walked me to where the cashier was seated and she in a fright just tossed the keys at me. We headed back to the till and he started emptying it. Unsatisfied by the amount he had bagged, he pointed the gun at my head and demanded more money. I tried to explain to him that what was there was all the nightshift cashing, but it's as if the more I tried to explain, the more I infuriated him. "I will shoot you; I will shoot you!!!" He roared.

I think in that moment I was in a state of shock because I had never experienced anything as terrifying. When he threatened to shoot me several times, I just stood there wondering if he was actually going to pull the trigger. Seeing that there nothing more they could possibly get from the restaurant the gunmen fled, but not before they had robbed dinning customers of their personal belongings.

A couple of minutes after they left, armed response arrived. They inspected the scene and took statements from shaken customers and the workers who had been on duty. It was all just protocol but 1 knew those tyrants had gotten away with it. There is a reason I survived that experience and lived to tell the story. I survived because of purpose. I may have just been a waitress at the time but the creator had mapped out in advance that 1 would some day write books and do what was destined for my life, and that is why I believe no one can kill your destiny.

There will be fierce opposition, distractions and detours on your path, but nothing can keep you from getting to the place preordained for you. You will end up right where God intended. I have this strong belief that I will fulfil all my purpose and what was written for my life. Destiny can be under attack, it can face resistance, but it cannot be destroyed.

I'm reminded of a dream 1 once had where 1 was driving on a road and there were roadworks ahead and couldn't pass through. I then had to take a different and longer route but still got to my destination. In life it is sometimes so, detours may cause delays and it may take a while to get to your desired place but you will get there.

The reason why that accident didn't kill you, why you survived that trauma, that heartache or beat cancer is all because of purpose and destiny. You can't kill destiny. Yes, you can frustrate it, detour it, deter it or compromise it; but you cannot kill it. Nobody can annul what God foreordained for you. The enemy can use adversity and detours to try blind you, he can use pain to try paralyze you and make you lose heart, but he cannot alter what has already been concluded by God. It is only by freewill that this can be changed. No human being or foreign power can stop or hinder what God predetermined for your life.

You can send me on a roller coaster ride, steal my time and try to keep me in oblivion but l will get to my destiny. If it is meant to be, it will surely be. I may get there later than everybody else but bottom line is, l will get there. Every life God intended for me to inspire, will be touched.

So as you get up to start over and begin again, do it with the revelation that nothing can alter what has already been settled by God.

CHAPTER 22

YOUR RESTORATION & RESTITUTION

A broken heart can hurt far worse than a broken leg. There is a spiritual suffering of the inner person that is just as real as the pain we feel in the body... Warren Wiersbe

A renowned life coach called off her wedding a few days before she was set to get married which came as a bewildering surprise to many. A fortnight from what could have been her forever, she discovered devastating news about her fiancé. The man she had entrusted as her heart keeper unforgivingly pierced it and left her bleeding. He had been with another woman countless times in their pre-purchased matrimonial house that she had spent months decorating and turning into a home for their happily ever after.

Calling every guest set to attend to apologize and explain why there won't be a wedding anymore must have been the hardest thing she had ever to do. The financial blow of calling the caterers and the wedding venue to cancel, as well as having to pay cancellation fee was a loss she had write off. Everything faltered as if it had already been written in the stars. The agony of heartbreak can sometimes feel like your heart is being sandpapered. Like you will never be able to feel again. Nothing was ever going to be the same for her.

When she shares her story, she calls herself a woman with *massive faith,* and that I believe is what makes her restoration extraordinary. She soon recovered, married the most wonderful man and was blessed with triplets at the age of forty. God made up for the wasted years in such an extraordinary way, he understood that because of the time she lost, carrying each baby for nine months separately would not have redeemed the time. So God did the miraculous and exceeded her expectations by giving her triplets. Her story alludes to the truth that, there is nothing behind you that can outdo your future. There is no one who can convince me that anything l lost yesterday cannot be replaced with better. If you can just give tomorrow a chance, it will surely bring better.

There was a time in my life when I was the girl with the good job, decent car and bachelor flat but l lost it all. I did not lose it because l was reckless, it was taken from me in such a painful and unfair way and there was nothing I could do about it. It is only human nature to always want to recover everything we may have lost. But who is going to account for everything you lost and everything that was taken from you? Who is responsible for your wasted years? I may have lost so much, but 1 believe in double blessings for all my troubles. I trust that there is a God who can restore everything good thing we lost.

Somehow, we have to believe that God can birth something extraordinary out of any great suffering. To truly believe that he is the chaos master with a touch of the fixer. We may not be able to explain why certain things happened, but God won't let it go to waste. The blessing has to be greater than the tragedy. God will buy back your dignity, honour, time, and missed opportunities.

YOUR RESTITUTION

There is no story that enthralls me like that of Joseph. Imagine a man who is betrayed, falsely accused and becomes a convicted criminal. A man paraded before the masses with the officials announcing; "this is the man who tried to defile Potiphar's wife." People must have booed him as he made his way to prison, some spitting on him, calling him a traitor and a repulsive human being. His name was dragged through the mud and he became the talk of the town for all the wrong reasons. Nobody wanted to associate with him or even have a glance of him. There was no coming back from this.

I can't even begin to imagine the feeling of helplessness he had to bear. He was weak, vulnerable and had no one to come to his defense. It was his walk through the valley, his walk of shame and his death moment. But just when people thought there was no one watching, here comes God the master of clap backs and totally flips the script. That very same man Joseph is paraded yet again, but this time when they present him, it is done with the utmost reverence. There was drumroll and the official announced, "here is your new prime minister, the most powerful man in the land, bow down to him, shout praises to him and give the honour that is due to him.

Can you imagine the look on people's faces especially the ones who taunted him and cat called him? I'm sure some even whispered, I wish I could have been kinder and respectful towards him. The very man they wrote off as a lost cause became the delight of the land. This time it was his walk of glory.

At times that is how life is, you are betrayed, hurt and broken but then God shows up and turns everything around for your favour. He gives you double honour right in the presence of the people that cut you down, made you bleed and broke you. In that moment it won't matter who lied, who said what, who pulled game on you and thought they would get away with it. When God is done, those who loathed you will be bowing at the soles of your feet. The story always ends in vindication.

CHAPTER 23

FIGHTING FOR YOUR FUTURE

In the year 2010 I sat under a sermon titled, "Fighting for your future" and it completely changed my life. At the time I was a waitress at a popular restaurant but desperately desired better for my life. At that particular restaurant I worked, there was no basic salary and I was solely surviving on tips. So, I really had to push myself to make ends meet. I would day dream of better days and would picture myself walking through an office strutting my heels. In my mind I had created the ideal life. The coffee, the aura, and the weekends off, I had it all figured out.

On that Sunday as the message was preached, there is one phrase that stuck with me which was; "Lord you are God." The pastor preached so fervently that in whatever circumstance you may find yourself in, you must rise up and declare; "Lord you are God." For the following weeks wherever I went I kept repeating it within myself. In one instance I was having such a terrible day at work, and as I walked through the restaurant floor almost on the verge of tears I whispered in my heart; "Lord you are God" with so much faith.

The weeks that were to follow completely blew my mind. I went from being a waitress to a conventional office job in one of the most beautiful office parks in the city. And there I was strutting my heels every morning and sipping on coffee with rusks. To this very day I find myself saying, "Lord you are God" in my weak moments.

I may not know what your current circumstance is, but time and again just whisper; "Lord you are God." And when you do so, you are fighting for your future.

We were never designed to live a life of chasing shadows. Fight for your future.

Psalms 100 vs 3

"Know that the Lord He is God."

Hope is not overrated. Without it, a man continues to exist but seizes to live. He has breath in his lungs but a dead soul.

CHAPTER 24

REST IN HOPE

THE WOMAN WHO GAVE ME A NEW NAME

One of my greatest blessings has been the people I meet when I get an opportunity to travel. They turn out to be the most humble and amazing people who speak greatness into my life. I have had the privilege of meeting so many wonderful people in my journey. One those people really left an imprint in my heart because she gave me a new name.

This lovely woman is someone l had shared my story with and passion for writing. A few weeks after meeting her, I received a lovely handcrafted card with a message that read:

Dear Princess

It was pleasurable and memorable meeting you and hearing your story. I think of your name being complete as Princess Esperanza (Princess Hope) as fitting you, as you spread your message and book of hope.

It goes without saying that 1 cried after reading that heartwarming note. It was a confirmation that 1 should no longer address myself by my circumstance or past. My new name became Princess Esperanza which is Spanish for Hope. My new name meant that hope would become my anchor going forward.

Hope is not overrated. Without it, a man continues to exist but seizes to live. He has breath in his lungs but a dead soul.

The slightest bit of hope makes you want to get up and face another day. That is why I would rather be a prisoner of hope than a prisoner of fear. So, on days when you feel weak and feeble, or those moments where you may feel unqualified to take on dreams before you; rest in hope. Trust that you can do it because God will help you. Faith is your best wager in a world full of uncertainty. Faith is your invisible substance to attain the great things you desire.

Hope is not overrated. Without it, a man continues to exist but seizes to live. He has breath in his lungs but a dead soul.

Hope is an anchor. [*Hebrews 6 vs19*]

CHAPTER 25

THERE IS A HEREAFTER

If you give up, it will never happen. Faith is everything... Steve Harvey

It is always at what seems to be the end that God swoops in and reminds you of His sovereignty and that there is a hereafter. To show you that no matter what the past was, you have to move on to what's next. After heartbreak, divorce, trauma or loss there is a life to be lived to capacity. Dear reader it is my desire that this book serves as a reassurance that the undesirable place you may find yourself in, is not the end. Where you may see the end, God sees a detour and the ability to begin again.

Your new strength will come from trusting God as well as believing that life can be good again. With God every experience no matter how tragic, somehow leads to His purpose for you and the life He designed for you. And so I have learnt to put a "but" at the end of every unpleasant experience. *But God will fix it. But God will comfort me. But God will make a way. But God will make it right.*

The valley is a walk through, I'm convinced that there is a coming out on the other side of every circumstance that life may throw at us. We were not designed to stay in the valley of adversity but rather to limp if we have to, till we see a shaft of light. There is a hereafter.

YOU CAN BEGIN AGAIN...

www.ingramcontent.com/pod-product-compliance
Lightning Source LLC
Chambersburg PA
CBHW061527050726
47593CB00002B/701